CONTENTS

Published by Smart Apple Media,
an imprint of Black Rabbit Books
P.O. Box 3263, Mankato, Minnesota 56002
www.blackrabbitbooks.com

Published by arrangement with
The Salariya Book Company Ltd

Cataloging-in-Publication Data is available
from the Library of Congress

Printed in the United States
At Corporate Graphics,
North Mankato, Minnesota

9 8 7 6 5 4 3 2 1

ISBN: 978-1-62588-355-1

The ancient world	6
Armies of the East	8
The Assyrian army	10
Age of the pharaohs	12
The Egyptian army	14
Shock tactics	16
Greek city-states	18
Greek warriors	20
War at sea	22
Age of conquest	24
The Romans	26
Enemies of Rome	28
The Roman army	30
Roman defenses	32
Training	34
Life in the legion	36
Into battle	38
Auxiliaries	40
Time line	42
Glossary	44
Index	45

Photographic credits
t=top b=bottom c=center l=left r=right

Ancient Art and Architecture Collection: 21tr, 37bl
The Art Archive/British Museum/Dagli Orti: 10
The Art Archive/Musée du Louvre/Dagli Orti: 14, 15
The Art Archive/Staatliche Glypohtek Munich/Dagli Orti (A): 35
Mark Bergin: 42
Bildarchiv Steffens/Bridgeman Art Library: 33
Bresslich and Foss: 40
David Stewart: 32, 34, 35, 36
Digital Stock/Corbis corporation: 6b, 7tl, 26
Doug Smith: 28tr, 36bl, 37c
E. Hobson/ Ancient Art and Architecture Collection: 17
Egyptian National Museum, Cairo/Bridgeman Art Library: 17b
John Foxx Images: 12, 18, 19
Louvre, Paris, France/Bridgeman Art Library: 7tr
Mountain High Map/copyright 1993 Digital Wisdom Inc: 6/7
Staatliche Museen zu Berlin – Preussicher Kulturbesitz,
  Antikerammlung/ bpk photo: Johanes Laurnetiiub, 2002: 211
Wadsworth Atheneum, Hartford/ J. Pierpont Morgan Collection/
  Joseph Szaszfai: 20

Every effort has been made to trace copyright holders.
The Salariya Book Co. apologises for any unintentional
omissions and would be pleased, in such cases,
to add an acknowledgement in future editions.

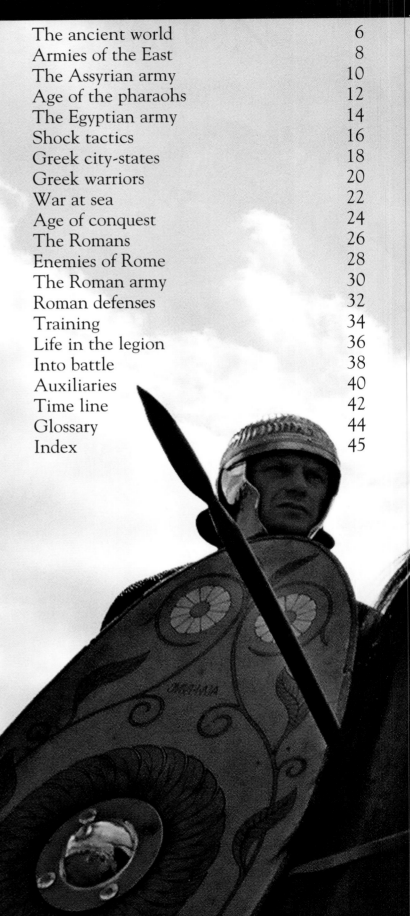

Warfare

in the

Ancient World

Written and illustrated
by Mark Bergin

A⁺
Smart Apple Media

THE ANCIENT WORLD

The first civilizations arose in the fertile lands around the major rivers of the Near East. As these societies grew they shared many common features: the development of government, writing, cities, and grand public buildings. Food production increased with irrigation so fewer people were needed for farming. This resulted in more people moving to towns and cities as craftsmen and traders. As the cities grew they became power bases for rulers. Central governments were created, controlling armies, trade, and food production. Legal systems were developed, and distinct classes began to form within society. As populations grew larger they came into conflict over land, trade routes, and resources.

THE ROMANS

The Romans established a republic in 510 B.C. that gradually expanded its power with the use of military force. They conquered the highly civilized Greeks to the east and brought civilization to the Celtic tribes of the north and west. The Romans dominated the western world for over 500 years (31 B.C. to 565 A.D.). Under *Pax Romana*—the Roman peace—law, order, and prosperity were brought to bear across the Empire.

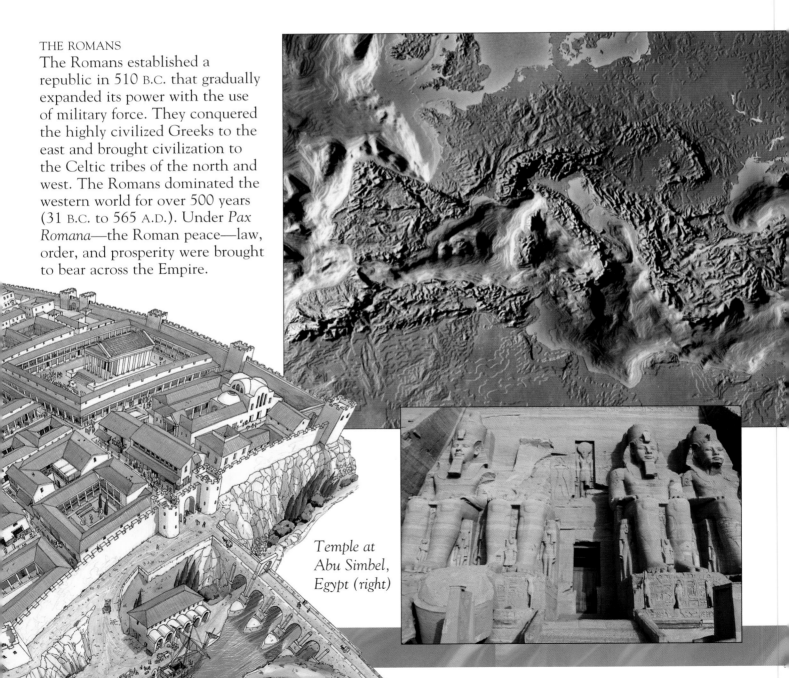

Temple at Abu Simbel, Egypt (right)

Parthenon, in Athens, Greece

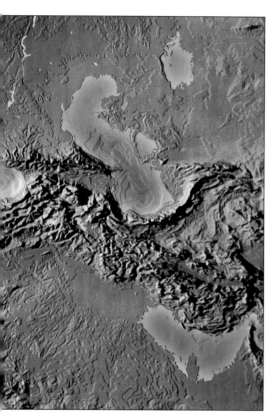

THE GREEKS

Greek power stemmed from the formation of city-states or *poleis*. These independent, self-governing communities fought for land and trade routes and against invasions by the expanding Persian Empire to the east. After the Peloponnesian War (431–404 B.C.) the Greek city-states were brought together by Alexander the Great.

THE PERSIANS

In 550 B.C., Cyrus, the prince of Persia, united the peoples of Medes and Persia to make Iran the dominant power in Asia and the Near East. Successful military campaigns increased his empire until it incorporated the Middle East, the Ionian Greek settlements of Asia Minor, Babylon, and Afghanistan. After about 100 years of stability, Persia was attacked and eventually defeated in 331 B.C. by the Greeks, who were led by Alexander the Great.

THE EGYPTIANS

The power of the ancient Egyptian civilization lasted for over 3,000 years. Successive pharaohs expanded out from the Nile valley into the Middle East and Asia with large, well-trained armies. By the Middle Kingdom (2040–1790 B.C.) large fortresses had been built to guard the frontiers of Egypt in the south and east.

THE ASSYRIANS

From around the 10th century B.C. to the 7th century B.C. the Assyrian Empire was the dominant military power in the Near East. At the height of its power, under King Ashurbanipal (668–627 B.C.), the Empire stretched from Egypt in the west to the borders of Iran in the east.

Sumerian chariot of King Eannatum of Lagash, c. 2500 B.C.

SUMERIAN CHARIOT
This lumbering four-wheeled chariot (below) was drawn by onagers (wild donkeys). Such chariots were probably used as troop carriers rather than fighting platforms.

ARMIES OF THE EAST

Power ebbed and flowed between various kingdoms as they fought over the region's fertile lands, trade routes, and gold and silver deposits. Some societies grew under strong leadership; others prospered through military skill. When several warring states were at last united by the King of Ur in 2500 B.C., they became known as the Sumerians. The Sumerians were the first civilization to use chariots and infantry in battle formation.

The Hittites, a people from the mountains of Armenia, had conquered Syria and Palestine by 1343 B.C. They used iron weapons, which gave them a great advantage over enemies still using bronze because iron is stronger than bronze. The Sumerians called iron *metal from Heaven* because of the advantages iron weapons had in battle.

The Syrians were at the height of their power in the 10th and 9th centuries B.C., until they split into warring kingdoms. The best known of these was Damascus.

This archer (below) has a triangular composite bow and distinctive, geometric patterned, clothing. This image is based on one seen on a vizier's tomb in Thebes, Egypt.

Shau-Bedouin

Syrian archer
The Shau-Bedouin had an alliance with the Libyans against the Egyptians. The warrior carries spears and a khopesh.

Semite archer

Sea Peoples warrior

Hittite guard

Libyan archer

Semites, also known as Israelites, occupied the region around Jordan and the Dead Sea. This archer (above) holds typical weapons—a bow and a duck-billed ax.

The Sea Peoples invaded Egypt in 1200 B.C. They were driven back by Rameses III and eventually settled in towns around Palestine.

This Hittite (above) wears the kilt of a royal guard. His crested helmet indicates his rank. Other Hittite soldiers wore long, short-sleeved tunics.

Libyan tribes were known for their military skill. They had many conflicts with the Egyptians but they also served as mercenaries in the pharaohs' armies.

HITTITE CHARIOT
War chariots were commonly used in battles between the Hittites and Egyptians. Each chariot had a three-man crew: a driver, a shield bearer, and an armored spear-man. Rameses II called the Hittites *humty* (women soldiers) due to the way they wore their hair.

Hittite chariot

THE ASSYRIAN ARMY

The organization, efficiency, and effectiveness of the Assyrian army had no equal until the rise of the legions of Rome. After suffering four centuries of domination by the Babylonian and Hittite empires, the Assyrian attitude to outsiders hardened. On battle campaigns they attacked their enemies, intent on extermination or forced resettlement. At its height, under King Ashurbanipal (ruled 668–627 B.C.), the Assyrian army must have struck terror into its opponents. The well-trained and well-armed force could field 20,000 foot soldiers, 12,000 cavalry, and 1,200 two-horse chariots. Their daggers and swords were made of iron—stronger weapons than those their opponents had. In sieges, the Assyrian force used six-wheeled assault towers each equipped with an iron-tipped battering ram. After King Ashurbanipal's death, the Empire collapsed under the rule of weaker kings and was once more taken over by the Babylonians.

ARMED FORCES
Assyrian archers, infantry and cavalry (opposite) all wore the same standard bronze-plate body armor and iron helmets. Warhorses were protected by tough fabric armor.

CAPTIVES
The Assyrians were ruthless in war. Their treatment of captives was notorious—they were impaled on stakes or flayed alive. When Assyrian King Shalmanaser planned to sell 10,000 enemy soldiers as slaves he first had them blinded.

This relief (left) discovered in Nimrud (present-day Iraq) shows an Assyrian attack on an enemy village.

Assyrian war chariots (right) were so heavy that each needed four horses to pull it. Such chariots proved to be decisive weapons in the battle at Halule in 691 B.C. After the demise of the Assyrian Empire, the chariot design was adopted by the Babylonian forces of Nebuchadnezzar II.

Heavy chariot of Ashurbanipal, 7th century B.C.

Archer

Infantryman
c. 655 B.C.

Cavalryman
c. 655 B.C.

AGE OF THE PHARAOHS

Ancient Egypt

*T*hrough the arid landscape of Egypt runs the River Nile. Every year the river overflows its banks, flooding the land on either side. This inundation brings life-giving water and rich riverbed nutrients to the soil, and it allowed the ancient Egyptians to grow food for themselves with enough left to export. The region was also rich in gold, copper, and quality building stone, and Egypt became wealthy.

For over 3,000 years, the kings of Egypt were given the title pharaoh, which translates to "great house." The ancient Egyptians believed that the pharaohs were living gods, and this was reflected in the construction of their fantastic tombs, the great pyramids. The pharaohs had supreme power, with governors and officials on hand to carry out their will. Pharaohs developed efficient and well-organized armies to expand Egypt's borders and protect against enemies.

PYRAMIDS
The three pyramids at Giza were built between 2660–2560 B.C. They were shaped to represent the sun's rays falling to earth—the dead pharaoh was believed to climb to heaven on these rays. The largest pyramid, constructed for Pharaoh Cheops, is the largest stone structure in the world at 482 ft. high.

Giza

Memphis

Border
fort

Bedouin tribes

River Nile

Western Desert

Eastern
Desert

Red Sea

Thebes

Karnak

Nubian
warriors

Valley of the Kings

Philae

THE EGYPTIAN ARMY

*I*n the New Kingdom period (1567–1085 B.C.) the ancient Egyptian army was well structured, with a strong chain of command. As a new recruit, a peasant volunteer or conscript was taken down the River Nile to a vast training camp near the city of Memphis. Here he was taught to march and learned skills such as fighting with a sword and shield, archery, understanding battle tactics, and chariot driving. Once their training was complete, recruits joined an army division.

WEAPONS
The khopesh (right) was a curved sword adopted by the Egyptians from the Hyksos. The Hyksos invaded and conquered parts of Egypt during the second intermediate period (1790–1550 B.C.). They also introduced scale armor, composite bows, and horse-drawn battle chariots to the Egyptians.

NUBIAN ARCHERS
Nubians (right) were mercenaries, professional soldiers employed by the pharaoh. They were valued for their skills as archers. Their chiefs wore ostrich feathers, large gold earrings, and collars as signs of their rank.

PYRAMID OF COMMAND
The pharaoh was the overall commander of the Egyptian army. His generals were division commanders, and beneath them were officers in control of smaller units. The army also needed skilled doctors, scribes, and priests.

An officer's rank was shown by his baton (below). The baton was also useful for disciplining recruits.

Officer

ARMY DIVISIONS
Every army division had about 145,000 men, 4,000 of whom were foot soldiers. The remaining 1,000 were charioteers who fought with bows and spears.

Nubian archers

DAILY PRACTICE
Wrestling (above) kept the soldiers fit and agile. Drilling and marching kept up discipline and stamina. Soldiers learned to act on trumpet signals to charge and retreat.

GUARDING THE EMPIRE
The fortification at Semnah (below) was built in the New Kingdom period as part of a line of forts designed to repel invasions from the Sea Peoples and the Libyans.

WEAPONS

By the New Kingdom, the blades of swords and axes were made of bronze—previously these weapons were made from stone and copper.

Ax

Ax head

Egyptian curved-blade ax c. 3000 B.C.

Bronze daggers with ivory decoration

Bronze daggers

SHOCK TACTICS

The fast, light, and maneuverable chariot became a devastating weapon in ancient Egypt. Introduced by the Hyksos, the Egyptians developed their own tactics for the best use of the chariots in battle. Chariots were used as mobile fighting platforms for archers, assaulting the enemy's front line from a distance and breaking up the infantry before Egyptian troops attacked.

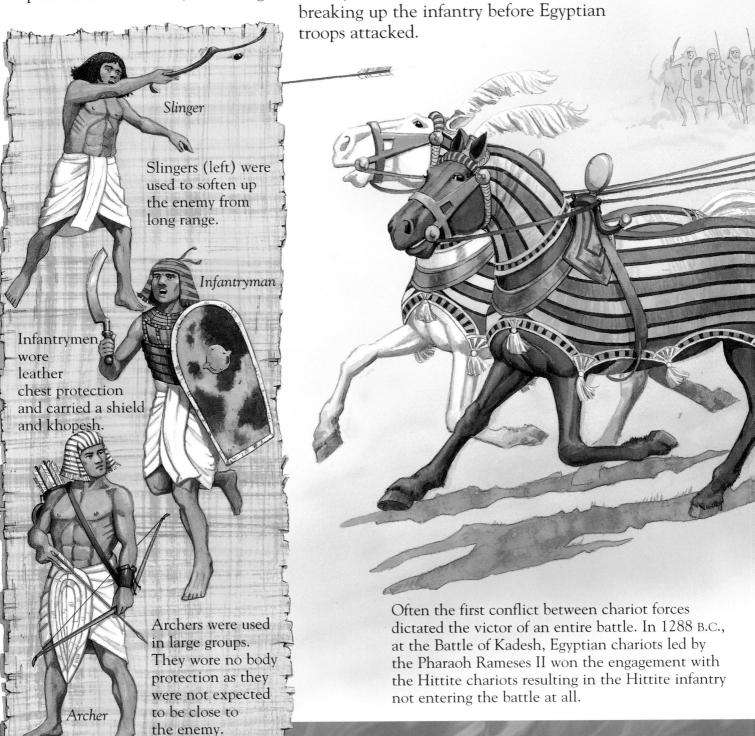

Slinger

Slingers (left) were used to soften up the enemy from long range.

Infantryman

Infantrymen wore leather chest protection and carried a shield and khopesh.

Archers were used in large groups. They wore no body protection as they were not expected to be close to the enemy.

Archer

Often the first conflict between chariot forces dictated the victor of an entire battle. In 1288 B.C., at the Battle of Kadesh, Egyptian chariots led by the Pharaoh Rameses II won the engagement with the Hittite chariots resulting in the Hittite infantry not entering the battle at all.

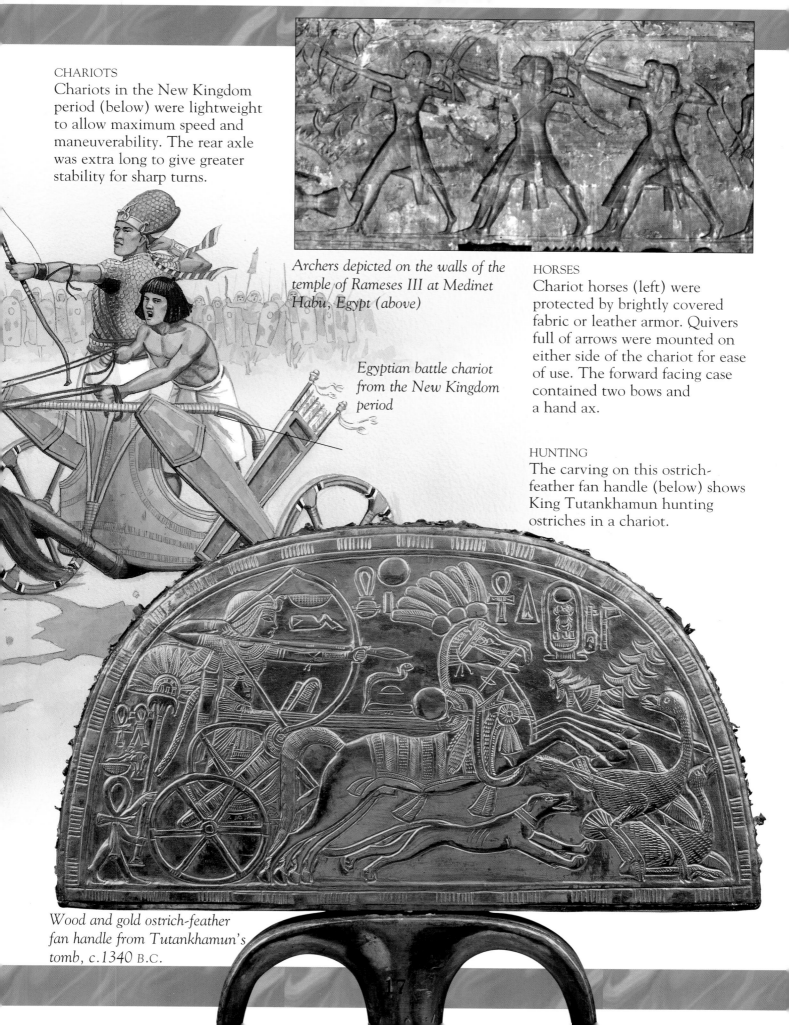

CHARIOTS

Chariots in the New Kingdom period (below) were lightweight to allow maximum speed and maneuverability. The rear axle was extra long to give greater stability for sharp turns.

Archers depicted on the walls of the temple of Rameses III at Medinet Habu, Egypt (above)

Egyptian battle chariot from the New Kingdom period

HORSES

Chariot horses (left) were protected by brightly covered fabric or leather armor. Quivers full of arrows were mounted on either side of the chariot for ease of use. The forward facing case contained two bows and a hand ax.

HUNTING

The carving on this ostrich-feather fan handle (below) shows King Tutankhamun hunting ostriches in a chariot.

Wood and gold ostrich-feather fan handle from Tutankhamun's tomb, c.1340 B.C.

GREEK CITY-STATES

Athena

*About 2,500 years ago the peoples of Greece formed the first great civilization in mainland Europe. Most ancient Greeks lived in communities known as *city-states*. Each city-state consisted of a small, self-governing city and the surrounding countryside that it controlled. There were many city-states in ancient Greece, and they were all fiercely independent. Each had its own fighting force, and conflicts were common due to their expanding populations and the shortage of good farmland. This resulted in some city-states becoming more powerful, particularly those of Athens and Sparta. In addition to internal conflict, the ancient Greeks suffered two invasions by the Persians. On both fronts, the Greeks fought hard campaigns, and defeated the Persians, forcing them to withdraw.

Between 447–438 B.C. the Athenians built the Parthenon (below). The temple was built as thanks to their goddess Athena (left) for their victory over the Persians.

The Parthenon

THE ASSEMBLY IN ATHENS
The golden age of Greek city-states such as Athens was between 479–431 B.C. Great progress was made in the sciences, the arts, sports, and politics. *Demokratia* is a Greek word meaning "rule of the people," and it was in the city-state of Athens that democracy was born. The Assembly in Athens met every nine days, and Athenian citizens could have their say and vote on important matters. About 5,000 citizens regularly attended, so Assembly meetings were often noisy and argumentative.

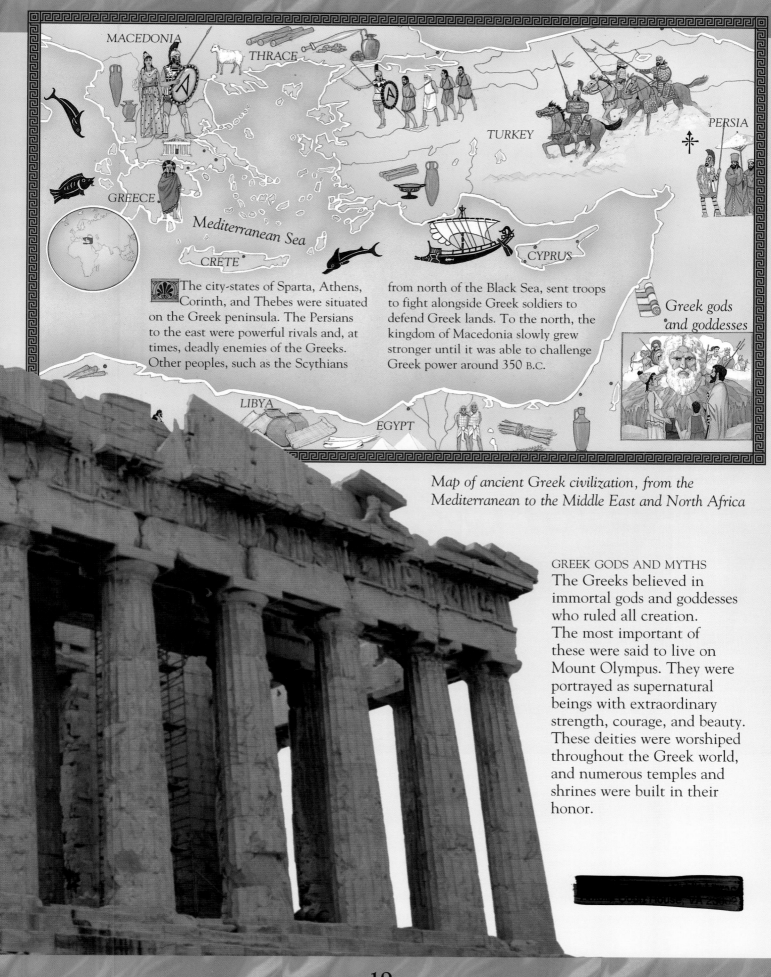

MACEDONIA

THRACE

TURKEY

PERSIA

GREECE

Mediterranean Sea

CRETE

CYPRUS

The city-states of Sparta, Athens, Corinth, and Thebes were situated on the Greek peninsula. The Persians to the east were powerful rivals and, at times, deadly enemies of the Greeks. Other peoples, such as the Scythians

from north of the Black Sea, sent troops to fight alongside Greek soldiers to defend Greek lands. To the north, the kingdom of Macedonia slowly grew stronger until it was able to challenge Greek power around 350 B.C.

Greek gods and goddesses

LIBYA

EGYPT

Map of ancient Greek civilization, from the Mediterranean to the Middle East and North Africa

GREEK GODS AND MYTHS
The Greeks believed in immortal gods and goddesses who ruled all creation. The most important of these were said to live on Mount Olympus. They were portrayed as supernatural beings with extraordinary strength, courage, and beauty. These deities were worshiped throughout the Greek world, and numerous temples and shrines were built in their honor.

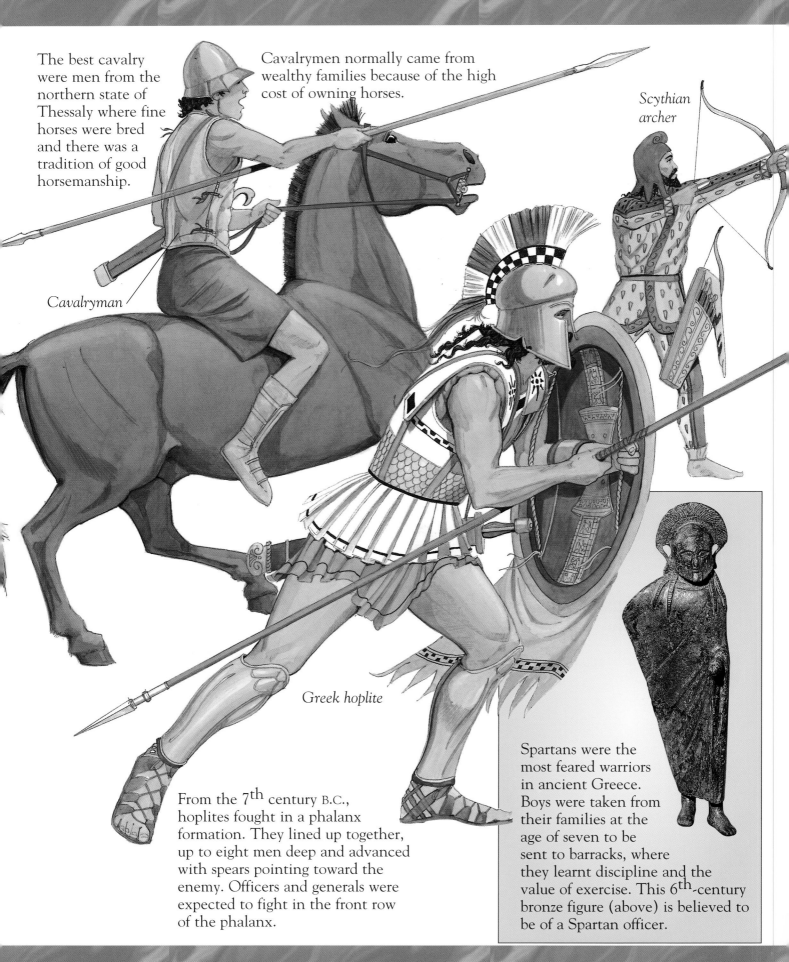

The best cavalry were men from the northern state of Thessaly where fine horses were bred and there was a tradition of good horsemanship.

Cavalrymen normally came from wealthy families because of the high cost of owning horses.

Scythian archer

Cavalryman

Greek hoplite

From the 7th century B.C., hoplites fought in a phalanx formation. They lined up together, up to eight men deep and advanced with spears pointing toward the enemy. Officers and generals were expected to fight in the front row of the phalanx.

Spartans were the most feared warriors in ancient Greece. Boys were taken from their families at the age of seven to be sent to barracks, where they learnt discipline and the value of exercise. This 6th-century bronze figure (above) is believed to be of a Spartan officer.

GREEK WARRIORS

Hoplites fought with long spears and swords. They held large round shields called argives and were protected by crested bronze helmets, breast plates, and greaves.

This bronze figure (below) portrays a typical hoplite, but his spear is missing. Notice the long hair flowing from under his helmet.

This Greek relief carving (above) shows hand-to-hand fighting. The warriors hold large bronze shields with grips around the rim.

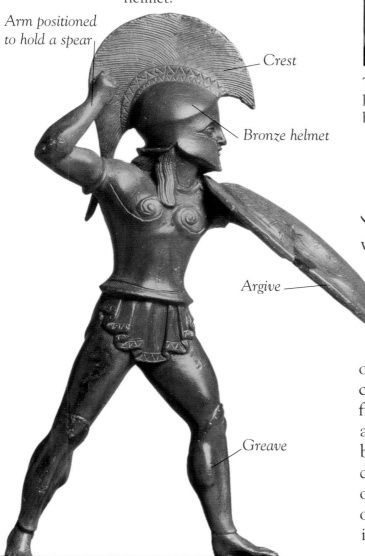

Arm positioned to hold a spear

Crest

Bronze helmet

Argive

Greave

Greek city-states were rivals for trade and land and were often at war. Sparta was dedicated to warfare—all its male citizens were soldiers, and the city was run like an army camp. The Athenians expected all male citizens over the age of 17 to defend their homeland, and when the government called them to fight it was regarded as a great honor. The majority of the Athenian army were foot soldiers called hoplites. They were mainly recruited from farming families wealthy enough to afford the necessary armor and weapons. On becoming a soldier they swore an oath, to defend "the wheat, the barley, the vines, the olives, and figs." Wars in this period were often short because men had to be home in time for the harvest—if crops were not harvested then the entire state suffered a lack of food.

WAR AT SEA

The Athenian navy played a vital part in Athen's empire-building around the Aegean Sea. The navy recruited over 20,000 free men, mostly those who could not afford the armor necessary to be a hoplite.

The three main types of Greek warships were known as penteconters, biremes, and triremes.

A penteconter was a galley with 50 oarsmen; biremes had two rows of oars, one above the other; and triremes had a total of 170 oarsmen. Triremes also had one large mast with a sail. Before a battle, the sail and rigging were taken down, and the trireme was powered by the oarsmen.

FIGHTING AT SEA
A trireme's fighting force were heavily armored hoplites (left). They boarded enemy ships or defended their own from the upper deck.

This vase decoration (far left) shows a bireme setting sail. At the stern are two steering oars and a ladder, used as a gangplank by the crew.

Hoplite

BATTLE OF SALAMIS

One of the most important Greek victories at sea was against the Persians at the Battle of Salamis in 480 B.C. The Greeks had only 300 triremes against 800 Persian ships. The Greek fleet retreated into narrow channels around the island of Salamis; the Persians followed, but their fleet was so large that there was no room to maneuver. The Greeks attacked the Persians, ramming their ships and forcing a retreat.

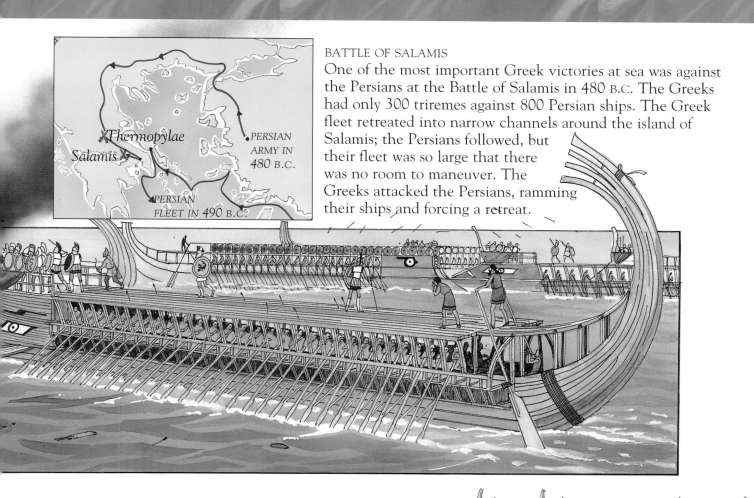

Thermopylae

Salamis

PERSIAN ARMY IN 480 B.C.

PERSIAN FLEET IN 490 B.C.

BATTLE TACTICS

A favored trireme tactic was to sail straight at the enemy amidships, ramming a hole and sinking the vessel. Triremes also sailed close alongside, smashing the enemy's oars with the bronze prow. This left the enemy ship helpless and vulnerable to boarding or ramming. A brazier was kept onboard Greek ships to set torches and arrows on fire. When fired at an enemy ship, the burning arrows and torches set the vessel alight, causing its crew to panic.

Trireme ramming another vessel with its bronze prow

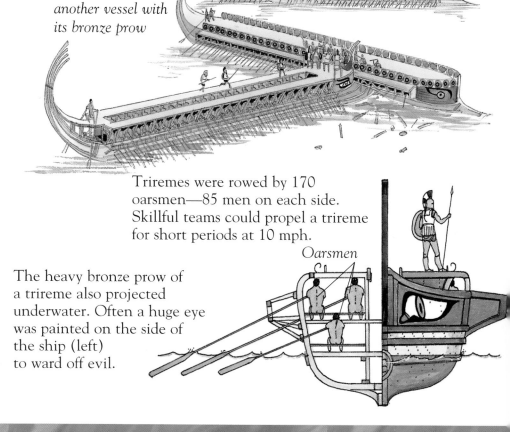

Triremes were rowed by 170 oarsmen—85 men on each side. Skillful teams could propel a trireme for short periods at 10 mph.

Oarsmen

The heavy bronze prow of a trireme also projected underwater. Often a huge eye was painted on the side of the ship (left) to ward off evil.

Prow

AGE OF CONQUEST

Alexander III became King of Macedonia, the most powerful state in Greece, in 336 B.C. Many Greek states were weakened after the long Peloponnesian War (431–404 B.C.). Alexander's father, Philip II, had seized the opportunity to make himself master of all Greece, but he was murdered at the height of his power. Alexander made the most of the power base left by his father and became the supreme military commander of his day, known as Alexander the Great. His speed and decisiveness made him an excellent general. He insisted on leading his men in battle, sharing the dangers and discomforts of campaigns, and this inspired loyalty from his men during the long years of his conquests. In 13 years, with only around 35,000 troops, Alexander defeated the vast Persian Empire, and conquered lands in Asia Minor, Egypt, and India.

Map of Alexander the Great's conquests 334–325 B.C.

Alexander finally destroyed the Persian army at the Battle of Gaugamela in 331 B.C. He went on to sweep through Egypt into India.

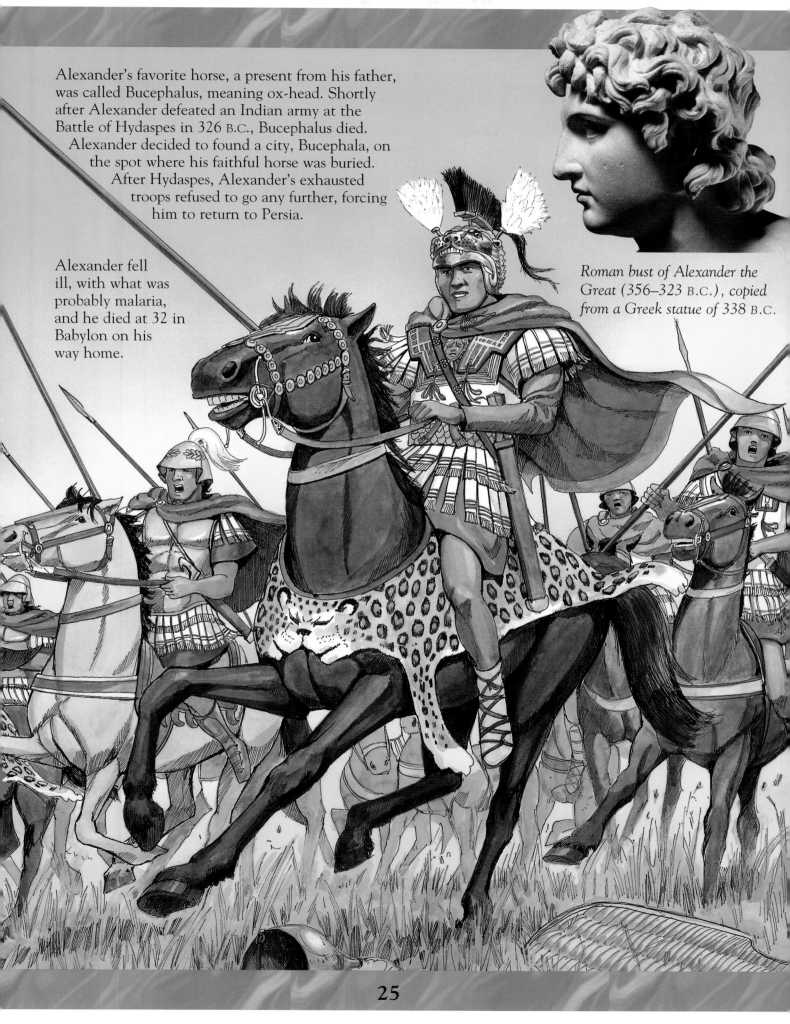

Alexander's favorite horse, a present from his father, was called Bucephalus, meaning ox-head. Shortly after Alexander defeated an Indian army at the Battle of Hydaspes in 326 B.C., Bucephalus died. Alexander decided to found a city, Bucephala, on the spot where his faithful horse was buried. After Hydaspes, Alexander's exhausted troops refused to go any further, forcing him to return to Persia.

Alexander fell ill, with what was probably malaria, and he died at 32 in Babylon on his way home.

Roman bust of Alexander the Great (356–323 B.C.), copied from a Greek statue of 338 B.C.

THE ROMANS

*A*round 510 B.C., Rome began to develop from a small town into a busy city. Roman citizens fought successfully to control vital trade routes throughout southern Italy and gained land. Rome's rise to power would have been impossible without an efficient, well-organized, and loyal army. Around 270 B.C., the army began to conquer neighboring regions, and by 50 B.C. Rome's generals had marched northwards and conquered much of Germania (present-day Germany) and Gaul (France). The Romans invaded Britain in 43 A.D. From 106–116 A.D. Rome overran the Middle East, and by 117 A.D. the Roman Empire encircled all of the Mediterranean Sea, covering large areas of Europe, the Near East, and Africa. All conquered lands sent goods and money to Rome as tribute and taxes. In return, the Empire provided a stable, relatively peaceful society, good laws, and profitable trade. Its professional army provided soldiers to man forts all around the frontiers, defending from attacking tribes and bordering kingdoms. Roman imperial power lasted almost five centuries until Rome was sacked in 410 A.D. by Alaric the Visigoth. The Empire finally collapsed around 476 A.D. when the last western emperor was deposed.

Map showing the Roman Empire

Londiniu

HISPANIA

Symbols of ancient Rome's power can still be seen today. All over the Empire the Romans created great structures, from the Colosseum (right) and Forum in Rome to the Pont du Gard in France and Hadrian's Wall in Britain. These structures provide an insight into the lives of the Romans, their government, and their conquests.

GERMANIA

GAUL

Roman Empire's
frontier

DACIA

Black Sea

ITALY

Rome

Naples

GREECE

Mediterranean Sea

Carthage

SICILY

CRETE

CYPRUS

AFRICA

EGYPT

ENEMIES OF ROME

Roman coin showing a barbarian on horseback

The Roman Empire met resistance from a variety of cultures and armed forces. By Roman standards the Germanic peoples of northern Germany were uncivilized, and the Romans called them "barbarians." The Germanic peoples lived in tribes and were always fighting among themselves for territory. This made it easier for the well-disciplined Roman soldiers to defeat them. In the 5th century B.C., present day France, Belgium, and Britain were inhabited by Celtic tribes, called *Galli* or Gauls. They were skilled metalworkers, but their iron weapons could not stop the Romans. By 51 B.C., Julius Caesar had conquered the whole area.

Germanic and Dacian (Romanian) warriors from the 1st –2nd century A.D.

A BARBARIAN VICTORY

Rome was not always victorious. In a battle at Teutoburger forest (western Germany) in 9 A.D. the barbarians destroyed three Roman legions. Following this defeat the Romans relied on a line of forts along the rivers Rhine and Danube to keep the barbarians at bay.

IBERIAN AND HISPANIC WARRIORS

The ancient peoples of the area now known as Spain were formidable warriors (left). They fought against Rome in the three Punic wars between 265–146 B.C. The Romans invaded because the land was fertile and rich in gold and silver deposits.

Iberian and Hispanic warriors, 2nd century B.C.

British chariots were extremely fast and maneuverable. Warriors could fight from the chariot or dismount to fight on foot. Fully-armed noblemen carried a shield, spear, and helmet.

Celtic chariot

Gallic warriors wore chain mail shirts over their tunics or sometimes fought naked! Some bronze helmets were decorated with boars or eagles, thought to give the wearer extra courage.

Horsehair crest

Gallic warriors

Parthian horse archer

The Parthians (left) were a nomadic people who conquered a large area of territory from Armenia to Afghanistan. One tactic the Parthians used was to gallop at the enemy's infantry in formation. About 300 ft. from the enemy, the riders wheeled around, shooting two or three arrows at the same time. This became known as a *Parthian shot*.

The Persians' (below) original homeland was northeast of the Persian Gulf. They conquered the Parthians in the 3rd century B.C. and went on to challenge the Roman Empire's frontier east of the Euphrates river.

Persian cavalryman

THE ROMAN ARMY

There were about 30 legions in the Roman army, made up of infantrymen and auxiliaries such as archers and cavalry. Each legion had its own name, number, badge, and command base or fort. Legions were posted throughout the Empire and were self-sufficient, each with their own commanders and ranking officers, ordinary soldiers and specialists, including doctors and engineers. In peacetime, soldiers trained and were put to work building forts and roads. The legions also acted as the local government in the regions where they were posted.

A LEGION
Every legion was divided into units and ranks. This meant that troops could be easily organized and controlled, and orders could be carried out quickly and efficiently.

Optio

Standard bearer

Centurion

Cavalry officer

A cohort was made up of six centuries. There were ten cohorts in a legion.

A century was 80 men (ten conturbeniums) commanded by a centurion.

Conturbeniums were the smallest units of the army, each consisting of eight men who cooked, ate, and shared a tent together.

CHAIN OF COMMAND
The legatus, or legate, was the commander of the legion. Below him were six officers, called tribunes, from Rome's most aristocratic families. Then came the praefectus castrorum or second-in-command. Under him was the primus pilus or chief centurion. Normal centurions each had a deputy called an optio, and at the bottom of the chain was the legionary. New recruits joined the army as legionaries and could work their way up to the rank of praefectus castrorum.

CHAIN OF COMMAND

Legatus

Tribunes

Praefectus castrorum

Primus pilus

Centurion

Optio

Legionary soldiers

Praefectus castrorum

Tribune

Legatus

Primus pilus

ROMAN DEFENSES

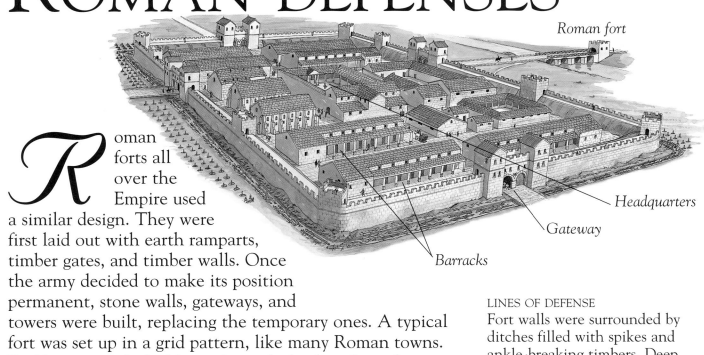

Roman fort

Headquarters

Gateway

Barracks

oman forts all over the Empire used a similar design. They were first laid out with earth ramparts, timber gates, and timber walls. Once the army decided to make its position permanent, stone walls, gateways, and towers were built, replacing the temporary ones. A typical fort was set up in a grid pattern, like many Roman towns. Buildings were linked by wide roads, leading from the headquarters in the middle of the fort to the commander's house and the four main gates. Barracks, granaries, storehouses, workshops, and a bathhouse were all contained within the fort's walls.

LINES OF DEFENSE
Fort walls were surrounded by ditches filled with spikes and ankle-breaking timbers. Deep holes were dug too, containing sharp stakes called *lilies*. These formed the first line of defense for forts in the most threatened areas, and the only way in was through the four guarded gateways.

Wooden spikes like this modern reconstruction (below) provided good defense against attacking soldiers and cavalry.

HEADQUARTERS

The headquarters (right) was the administrative and ceremonial center of the fort. A paved courtyard was surrounded by offices and a verandah. This led to an inner room where the legion's standards and a shrine were kept. Beneath this was a strongroom where soldiers' savings, valuables, and the legion's weapons and armor were stored. The largest room in the headquarters was a hall, where parades took place on special occasions and where the commander could address his troops.

TRAJAN'S COLUMN

This 98 ft.-high column in Rome was created in 113 A.D. to honor Emperor Trajan's victories in central Europe. It is covered in carvings of soldiers fighting and building forts. In this detail (below) troops are pictured digging foundations and building the walls of a fort.

Room containing standards and shrine

Courtyard and veranda

TRAINING

New recruits in training

Even when not on campaign, the Roman army continually practiced drills and tactics. Many Roman forts had a large open space within their walls, close to the headquarters building. This was used as an area where parades and kit-inspections regularly took place. Parades on important occasions were particularly elaborate and were opportunities for new recruits to learn discipline and recognize battle commands. New recruits also took part in daily weapons practice, using wooden swords and wicker shields (right). Long marches carrying heavy loads and building camps and forts helped keep soldiers fit for battle.

Reconstruction of a Roman practice shield

SHIELDS
The Romans used their shields to crash into opponents. Then they stabbed their opponents repeatedly with their sword or gladius. This meant that shield practice was an important part of training.

Wicker

Hide

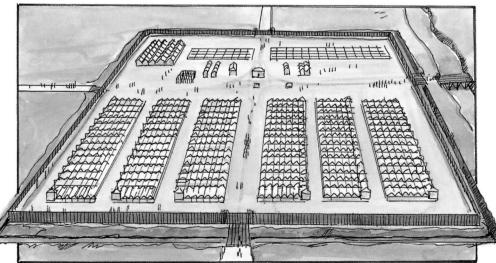

Marching camp

MARCHING CAMPS
On well-made Roman roads, heavily-laden soldiers could march about 25 mi. in a day. They sheltered overnight in temporary marching camps. These were always laid out in the same way as a fort, with the commander's tent in the center. A camp for an entire legion needed 800 tents. Half the legion stood on guard while the others dug a ditch and earth rampart all around the camp.

Reconstruction of a Roman tent and the results of a successful hunt

TENTS AND FOOD

When on the march, each soldier carried enough food for three days. They ate mostly bread, cheese, lentils, and beans, but this could be supplemented by rabbits and other animals from a hunt (above). Army tents were made of leather stretched over wooden poles. Eight men shared each tent.

BATTLE FORMATIONS

Practicing battle tactics and shield formations were an important element of the Roman army's success. When attacking fortifications, troops would move into the tortoise position, or *testudo* (right). They could protect themselves from the arrows and missiles raining down on them by interlocking their shields above their heads. A wedge-shaped formation called the *pig's head*, or *caput porcinum*, was used to thrust into enemy lines and crush them with a wall of shields.

Centurion

Reconstruction of a testudo

LIFE IN THE LEGION

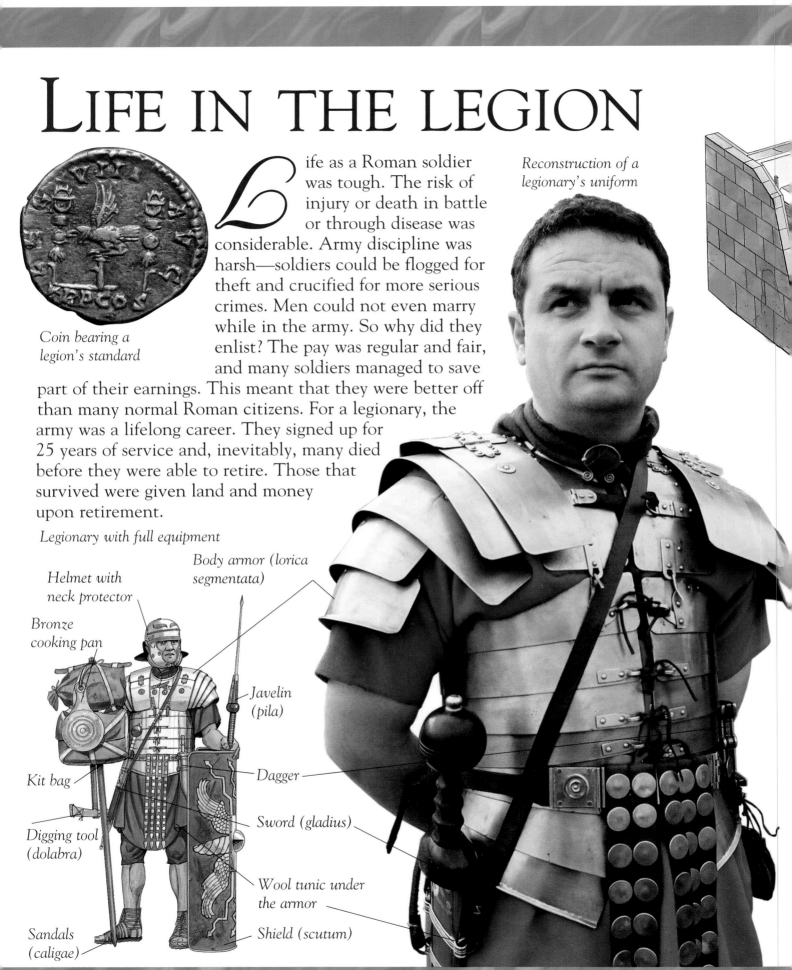

Life as a Roman soldier was tough. The risk of injury or death in battle or through disease was considerable. Army discipline was harsh—soldiers could be flogged for theft and crucified for more serious crimes. Men could not even marry while in the army. So why did they enlist? The pay was regular and fair, and many soldiers managed to save part of their earnings. This meant that they were better off than many normal Roman citizens. For a legionary, the army was a lifelong career. They signed up for 25 years of service and, inevitably, many died before they were able to retire. Those that survived were given land and money upon retirement.

Coin bearing a legion's standard

Reconstruction of a legionary's uniform

Legionary with full equipment

Helmet with neck protector

Body armor (lorica segmentata)

Bronze cooking pan

Javelin (pila)

Kit bag

Dagger

Digging tool (dolabra)

Sword (gladius)

Wool tunic under the armor

Sandals (caligae)

Shield (scutum)

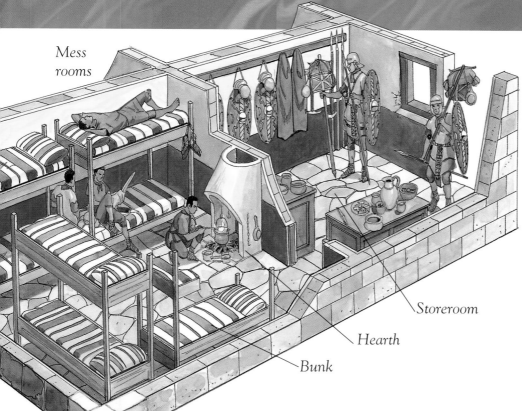

Mess rooms

Storeroom

Hearth

Bunk

BARRACKS AND MESS ROOMS

Each barrack block in a fort contained ten pairs of rooms called messes (left). Eight men shared each pair of rooms. In one were bunks where the soldiers slept, and there may have been a small hearth for warmth. The other room was used to store clothing, armor, equipment, and personal possessions. There was also an area for preparing food.

PAY DAY

Legionaries were paid about 225 denarii (silver pieces), and auxiliaries were paid 150 denarii per year in the 1st century A.D. Pay could be deducted if a unit had appeared cowardly in battle, and soldiers could be put on half pay for a year as punishment for serious offenses.

Roman centurion helmet with eagle decoration

Denarius coin depicting the Roman Emperor Nero

HELMETS

Roman helmets (left) were a sign of a solder's rank and were vital protection against enemy blows in battle.

TIME OFF

There was probably not a lot of free time for Roman soldiers. They could relax playing dice, cleaning armor, mending equipment, and taking turns cooking. Swords and daggers were sharpened and helmets polished. Gaming boards have been found in several Roman forts with counters made of stone, glass, or pottery.

INTO BATTLE

Typical Roman battle formation

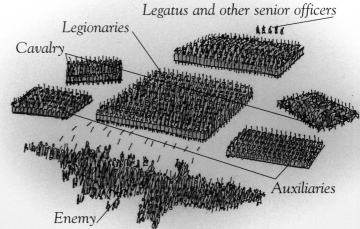

Cavalry
Legionaries
Legatus and other senior officers
Auxiliaries
Enemy

A ncient Rome was wealthy and could afford to keep a large permanent army. They could also build the roads and ships necessary to send forces all over the Empire, wherever and whenever they were needed.

There were about 150,000 legionaries in the army, and they proved to be a well-drilled and disciplined force in battle. They formed tight ranks and acted as a single force, legionaries to the front and center, reserve troops behind them. The auxiliary soldiers (see page 40) flanked either side. Moving towards the enemy, legionaries threw their javelins at a range of 82 ft. Then, protected by their shields, they advanced, engaging the enemy at close quarters with swords and daggers. Most of the forces encountered by the Romans were not so well trained or disciplined, and this assured Rome of success in extending its Empire.

BATTLE TACTICS

Roman commanders had an almost scientific approach to war. They did not believe in wasting their men in headlong charges at the enemy; instead, they considered the layout of the battlefield, direction of the wind, and even the time of day. Julius Caesar, one of Rome's most successful generals, advised his soldiers to attack when the sun was behind them, so that its rays would dazzle and confuse the enemy.

Onagers were used against enemy fortifications. On one end of the large arm was a sling containing rocks.

A counterweight was dropped at the other end of the onager, pivoting the arm and launching the rocks.

Two men were needed to operate a ballista (below): one to winch and the other to load and fire the large crossbow.

SIEGES
The Roman army was expert at siege warfare, using onagers, seige towers, catapults, and ballistas to pound enemy fortifications and city walls.

Onager

Ballista

Aquilifer

Imago standard bearer

Signifer

Cornicen

STANDARD BEARERS
As the legionaries went into battle, there were soldiers among them whose job it was to be seen rather than to fight. These were the standard bearers (right). They often wore animal skins over their heads to make them look more ferocious and imposing. It was seen as the greatest disgrace to lose your standard to the enemy in battle, so these men were well protected by soldiers willing to lay down their lives for the standard.

An aquilifer was the most important standard bearer as his standard showed the imperial eagle, or *aquila.*

A signifer wore a bearskin and a shirt of brass scales. He was the standard bearer for a century of legionaries.

The imago was a standard showing the emperor's head on it, a symbol of his presence and to keep up morale.

A cornicen was a horn player who gave signals during battle.

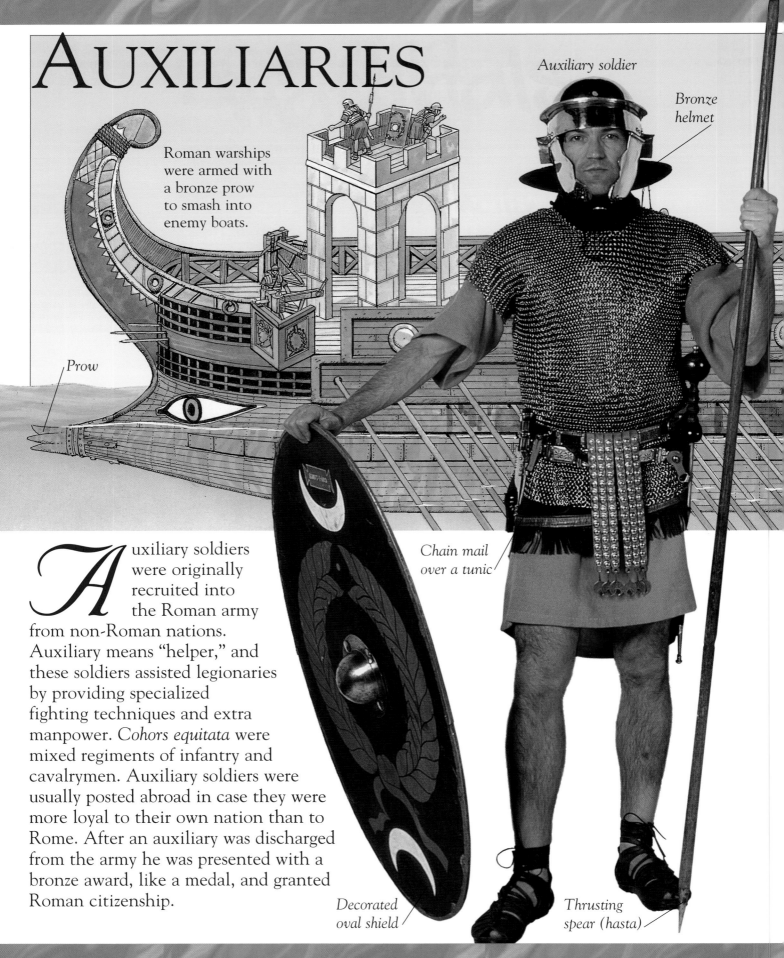

AUXILIARIES

Auxiliary soldier

Roman warships were armed with a bronze prow to smash into enemy boats.

Prow

Bronze helmet

Chain mail over a tunic

Decorated oval shield

Thrusting spear (hasta)

Auxiliary soldiers were originally recruited into the Roman army from non-Roman nations. Auxiliary means "helper," and these soldiers assisted legionaries by providing specialized fighting techniques and extra manpower. *Cohors equitata* were mixed regiments of infantry and cavalrymen. Auxiliary soldiers were usually posted abroad in case they were more loyal to their own nation than to Rome. After an auxiliary was discharged from the army he was presented with a bronze award, like a medal, and granted Roman citizenship.

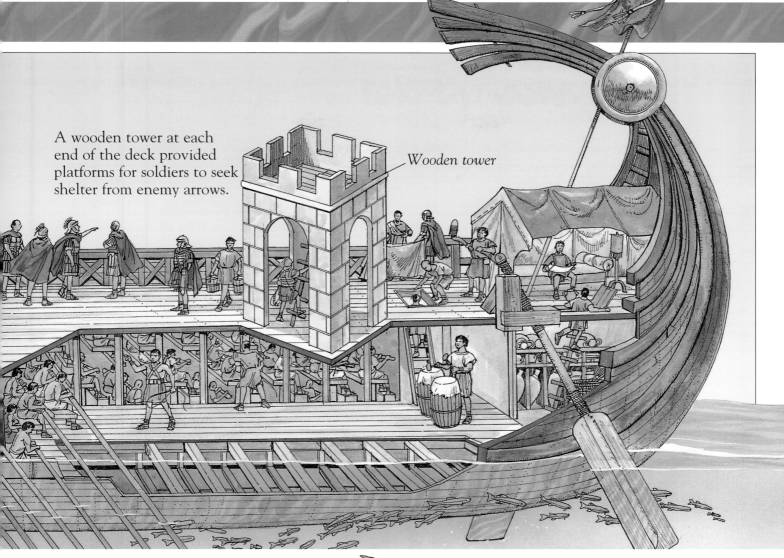

A wooden tower at each end of the deck provided platforms for soldiers to seek shelter from enemy arrows.

Wooden tower

ROMAN WARSHIPS

In 54 B.C., Julius Caesar had 600 special landing craft and 28 warships built for the invasion of Britain. These vessels were wider and lower so they could be loaded quickly and carry troops right onto the beaches.

AUXILIARY WEAPONS AND TECHNIQUES

Many of the auxiliary weapons and fighting techniques were adapted from their native lands. Horseback warriors came from conquered tribes in Gaul (France). Most auxiliary archers originated in the Middle East. Slingshot experts armed with lethal stone "bullets" came from the southern Mediterranean.

AUXILIARY CAVALRY

Auxiliary cavalry were known as *alae*, or wings, because they were fast-moving and fought on either side of the foot soldiers. They also served as scouts and escorts for convoys.

Auxiliary cavalryman

Saddle with four corners to hold the rider in place

TIME LINE

3100 B.C.
Upper and lower Egypt are unified by Menes, founder of the first Egyptian dynasty in Memphis.

2700 B.C.
The Sumerian/Egyptian culture starts to grow. The Sumerians use four-wheeled carts drawn by donkeys in warfare for the first time, around 2500 B.C.

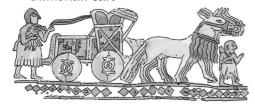

Sumerian cart

2682–2181 B.C.
Old Kingdom period of Egypt.

2400 B.C.
Rise of Canaanite power based in Ebla (Syria).

2040–1786 B.C.
Middle Kingdom period of Egypt. The nation is reunited and now centered in Thebes.

2100 B.C.
The Sumerian civilization is at its height.

1576 B.C.
The Hyksos are driven out of Egypt. Nubia (northern Sudan) is conquered by the Egyptians.

1567–1085 B.C.
New Kingdom period of Egypt.

1475 B.C.
The Hittites and Egyptians come into conflict over Palestine and Syria.

1375 B.C.
The Hittites expand and overrun the Babylonian Empire up to Syria.

1320–1200 B.C.
Pharaoh Seti I and Pharaoh Rameses II repel the Hittite threat and maintain Egyptian power.

Statue of Rameses II

1273 B.C.
The Hittites and Assyrians go to war resulting in the decline of the Hittite Empire.

1200 B.C.
The Sea Peoples invade Cyprus, Palestine, and Syria. They are halted on the borders of Egypt around 1190 B.C., by Rameses III. The Hittite Empire falls apart under the invasion of the Sea Peoples.

1100 B.C.
The pharaohs' powers are in decline, and the Egyptian military splits the Empire into small states.

900–750 B.C.
Rise of the Greek city-states.

Ancient Greek shield, sword, and helmet

509 B.C.
Founding of the republic of Rome.

546–449 B.C.
The Persian Wars. The Persians try to invade Greece but are driven back at the battle of Salamis in 480 B.C.

477–405 B.C.
The golden age of Athens as a Greek city-state.

446–404 B.C.
The Peloponnesian War between Athens and Sparta. The turning point was the siege of Syracuse in 415 B.C. when the Spartans helped the troops of Syracuse to defeat the Athenian navy.

382–336 B.C.
Weakness of the Greek city-states allows Philip II of Macedonia the opportunity to make himself master of Greece.

334–332 B.C.
The conquests of Alexander the Great. His last great battle, at Hydaspes in 326 B.C., is against the Indian King Porus. The king uses elephants in his forces, and Alexander is so impressed by them he eventually incorporates them into his own army.

Statue of Alexander the Great

146 B.C.
The Romans destroy Corinth and make Greece and Macedonia into one province.

73–71 B.C.
Spartacus, an ex-gladiator, leads a slave revolt over their harsh treatment. After several months, the rebellion is crushed by Roman General Pompey. The captured rebels are crucified along the length of the Appian way, a road leading to Rome.

59–51 B.C.
Julius Caesar wars with the Gauls in France. The Gauls adapt well to being conquered, and many take on Roman ways and learn Latin. Eventually the Gauls are allowed to govern themselves and become trusted allies of Rome.

55 B.C.
Julius Caesar leads an unsuccessful invasion of Britain.

49 B.C.
Julius Caesar marches into Rome to take control of the Empire and goes on to defeat Pompey's armies in Greece, Egypt, Asia, and Spain.

44 B.C.
Julius Caesar is murdered outside the Senate House in Rome.

44–31 B.C.
Civil war in the Roman Empire between Consul Octavian and one of the Roman leaders, Mark Anthony. Anthony is defeated by Octavian and his admiral Agrippa in the harbor at Actium (in present-day Greece).

27 B.C.
Octavian is renamed Augustus and becomes the first Roman Emperor.

Emperor Augustus

4 A.D.
Probable date of the birth of Jesus Christ.

9 A.D.
Germanic tribes destroy three Roman legions in the forest of Teutoburger, stopping Rome's advance across the Rhine.

43 A.D.
Under the orders of Emperor Claudius, the Roman army invades Britain.

61 A.D.
Boudicca, a tribal queen, leads a rebellion in eastern Britain but it is defeated by the Romans.

101–107 A.D.
Emperor Trajan goes to war in Dacia (Romania).

122 A.D.
Emperor Hadrian builds a huge fortified wall across the north part of Britain.

286 A.D.
Emperor Diocletian reforms the Roman army and splits the Empire into east and west. Each is ruled by an emperor and his junior but in 305-337 A.D. these power sharing arrangements break down.

312 A.D.
Emperor Constantine becomes the Roman Empire's single ruler. The Empire becomes Christian after Constantine's conversion in 313 A.D.

407 A.D.
Last Roman troops withdraw from Britain.

410 A.D.
The fall of Rome after it is sacked by Alaric, King of the Visigoths.

Fall of Rome

GLOSSARY

Argive A type of shield carried by a Greek infantryman.

Ballista A giant crossbow.

Baton A short stick carried to use as a weapon.

Battering ram A heavy beam used to batter down gates and walls during a siege.

Centurion A Roman army officer in charge of a century.

Century A unit in the Roman army consisting of eighty men.

Chain mail Flexible armor made of joined metal links or scales.

Chariot A horse-drawn vehicle used to carry soldiers in battle.

City-states Independent cities and the surrounding areas over which their governments rule.

Civilization A society governed by cultural and political ideals.

Cohort One of ten divisions which made up a Roman legion.

Conscript Someone who is forced to fight in an army.

Consul One of the two highest officials elected each year to rule over the republic of Rome.

Conturbenium The smallest unit in the Roman army, consisting of eight men.

Empire A collection of peoples and territories under the rule of a single person or state.

Greave A piece of armor that protects the shin from the knee to the ankle.

Hoplite A member of the Greek infantry.

Humty The name given to the long-haired Hittite warriors. It means "women soldiers".

Infantry Soldiers who fight on foot with carried weapons.

Khopesh An Egyptian curved sword.

Legion The largest unit in the Roman army, consisting of around 4,800 men.

Mercenaries Men hired and paid to fight for a foreign army.

Nomadic A people or tribe who move from place to place to find food.

Peloponnesian War A war from 431–404 B.C. in which the ancient Greek city-state of Athens was defeated by a group of rival states.

Phalanx A battle formation used by the ancient Greeks and Macedonians. It consisted of hoplites pointing spears out from a wall of overlapping shields.

Prow The front part of a ship's hull.

Onager (1) A wild donkey found in Central Asia.

Onager (2) A large siege engine used to hurl rocks.

Pharaoh The title of ancient Egyptian kings.

Poleis The Greek word for "city-state".

Punic Wars The three wars (264–241 B.C., 218–201 B.C. and 149–146 B.C.) in which ancient Rome defeated and eventually destroyed Carthage.

Quiver A case for arrows.

Rampart A fortification consisting of a steep bank, often topped with a fence or wall.

Regiment A group of soldiers under one commander.

Republic A state in which the people or their elected representatives hold power.

Scribe A person employed to write down what is spoken by his or her employer.

Siege The surrounding and blockading of a fortification or town in order to capture it.

Slinger Someone who uses a sling to hurl projectiles.

Tunic A loose-fitting garment extending to the knees.

Tribute A payment from one state to another.

Vizier A high officer in Muslim government.

INDEX

Page numbers in bold refer to illustrations

A

Alaric the Visigoth 26, 43
Alexander the Great 7, 24-25, **25**, 43, **43**
archers 8-9, **8-9**, 10, **11**, 14, **14**, 16, **16-17**, 30, 38, **38**, 41
armor 10, 14, 21, 22, 33, **36**, 37
Ashurbanipal, King of Assyria 7, 10
Assyrians 7, 10-11, **10-11**, 42
Athens 18-19, 22
  Assembly 18

B

Babylonian Empire 10, 42
barbarians 28, **28**
barracks 20, 32, 37, **37**
Britain 26, 28, 41, 43

C

Caesar, Julius 28, 38, 41, 43
cavalry 10-11, **11**, 20, **20**, 29, 30, **30**, 38, 40-41, **41**
Celtic tribes 6, 28, **29**
chain mail 29, 40, **40**, 44
chariots 8-9, **8-9**, 10-11, **11**, 14, 16-17, **17**, 29, **29**, 44
city-states, Greek 7, 18-19, 21, 42, 44
copper 12
Corinth 19, 43

D

Dacian warriors 28, **28**
discipline 14, 20, 28, 34, 36, 38

E

Egypt 6-7, 8-9, 12-13, **13**, 14, 24, 42-43
Egyptians 6-7, 8-9, 12-13, 14-15, **14-15**, 16-17, **16-17**, 42

F

farming 6, 18, 21
food 6, 12, **35**, 37
foot soldiers 10, 14, 21, 41
forts 14, 26, 28, 30, 32-33, **32**, 34, 37

G

Gaugamela, battle of 24
Gauls (Galli) 28-29, **29**, 43
Germanic peoples 28, **28**, 43
gladius 34, **36**
gods 12, 19, **19**
gold 12, 8, 28

[G column 2]

governments 6, 21, 26, 30
Greece 18-19, 42-43
Greeks 6, 18-19, 20-21, **20-21**, 22-23, 24-25, 43

H

Halule, battle of 11
helmets 9, 10, 20-21, **20-21**, 29, **29**, 36-37, 40, **40**, 42, **42**
Hispanic warriors 28, **28**
Hittites 8-9, **9**, 10, 16, 42
Hoplites 20-21, **20-21**, 22, **22**, 44
Hydaspes, battle of 24, 43
Hyksos 14, 16, 42

I

Iberian warriors 28, **28**
infantry 8, 10, **11**, 16, **16**, 29, 30, 40

K

Kadesh, battle of 16
khopesh 8, 14, **14**, 16, 44

L

Libyans 8-9, **9**, 14
lilies 32

M

Macedonia 19, 24, 42-43
Memphis, Egypt 14, 42
mercenaries 9, 14, 44

N

Nebuchadnezzar II, Babylonian ruler 11
Nile, river 7, 12, 14
Nubians 14, **14**

P

Parthians 29, **29**
Peloponnesian War 7, 24, 42
Persians 7, 18, 19, 23, 24-25, 29, **29**
phalanx 20, 44
pharaohs 9, 12, 14, 16, 42, **42**
Philip II, King of Macedonia 24, 42

R

Rameses II 9, 16, 42, **42**
Rameses III 9, 17, 42
ranks, within armies 14, 30-31, **31**, 37
Roman Empire 6, 10, 26-27, **27**, 28, 30, 32, 38, 40-41, 42, 43
Roman army

[R column 3]

aquilifer 39, **39**
auxiliary soldiers 30, 37, 38, 40-41, **40**
centurions 30-31, **30-31**, 44
chain of command 30-31, **30-31**
cohorts 31
conterbeniums 31
cornicen 39, **39**
forts 32-33, **32-33**
legionary soldiers 31, **31**, 36, **36**, 38, **38**, 40
legions 28, 30-31, **30**, 33, 34, 36-37, 43, 44
marching camps 34, **34**
signifer 39, **39**
standard bearers 30, **30**, 39, **39**

S

Salamis, battle of 23, 42
Scythians 19, 20
Sea Peoples 9, **9**, 14, 42
Semites (Israelites) 9, **9**
Semnah, fortification at 14, **14**
Shau-Bedouin 8, **8**
shields 16, **16**, 20-21, **20-21**, 29, 34-35, **34-35**, 36, 38, 40, **40**, 42, **42**
sieges 10, 39, 42, 44
silver 8, 28
slingers 16, **16**
Sparta 18, 19, 20-21, 42
Sumerians 8, **8**, 42
Syrians 8, 38

T

tactics 14, 16, 23, 34-35, 38
Teutoburger forest, battle of 28, 43
Thebes 19, 42
trade 6, 7, 8, 26
Trajan, Roman Emperor 33, 43
Tutankhamun, King of Egypt 17

V

Vizier 8, 44

W

wages 37
warships 22-23, **22-23**, 40-41, **40-41**
weapons
  bronze 8, 15, **15**
  Egyptian 8, 14-15, **14-15**
  Greek 21, **21**
  iron 8, 10, 28
  Roman 33, 34, 36, **36**, 38-39, **39**, 42